MY BODY, MY VOICE

THIS BOOK BELONGS TO:

For Nandi, who taught me the power of words – N.G.

For Nore, Kobe, Fien, Fijs & Elin—My favourite nieces and nephews – I.D.

Scholastic Press
An imprint of Scholastic Australia Pty Limited
(ABN 11 000 614 577)
PO Box 579 Gosford NSW 2250
www.scholastic.com.au

Part of the Scholastic Group
Sydney · Auckland · New York · Toronto · London · Mexico City
New Delhi · Hong Kong · Buenos Aires · Puerto Rico

Published by Scholastic Australia in 2025.

A catalogue record for this book is available from the National Library of Australia

ISBN: 978-1-76152-164-5

Typeset in Might Could Pencil and Fink.
Book design by Laura Ye.

Inge Daniels created these illustrations digitally.

We acknowledge the Traditional Owners of the Country on which we live and work.
We pay respect to Elders past and present.

Printed in China by RR Donnelley.
Scholastic Australia's policy, in association with RR Donnelley, is to use papers that are renewable and made efficiently with wood from responsibly managed sources, so as to minimise its environmental footprint.

10 9 8 7 6 5 4 3 2 1 25 26 27 28 29 / 2

A Scholastic Press book from Scholastic Australia

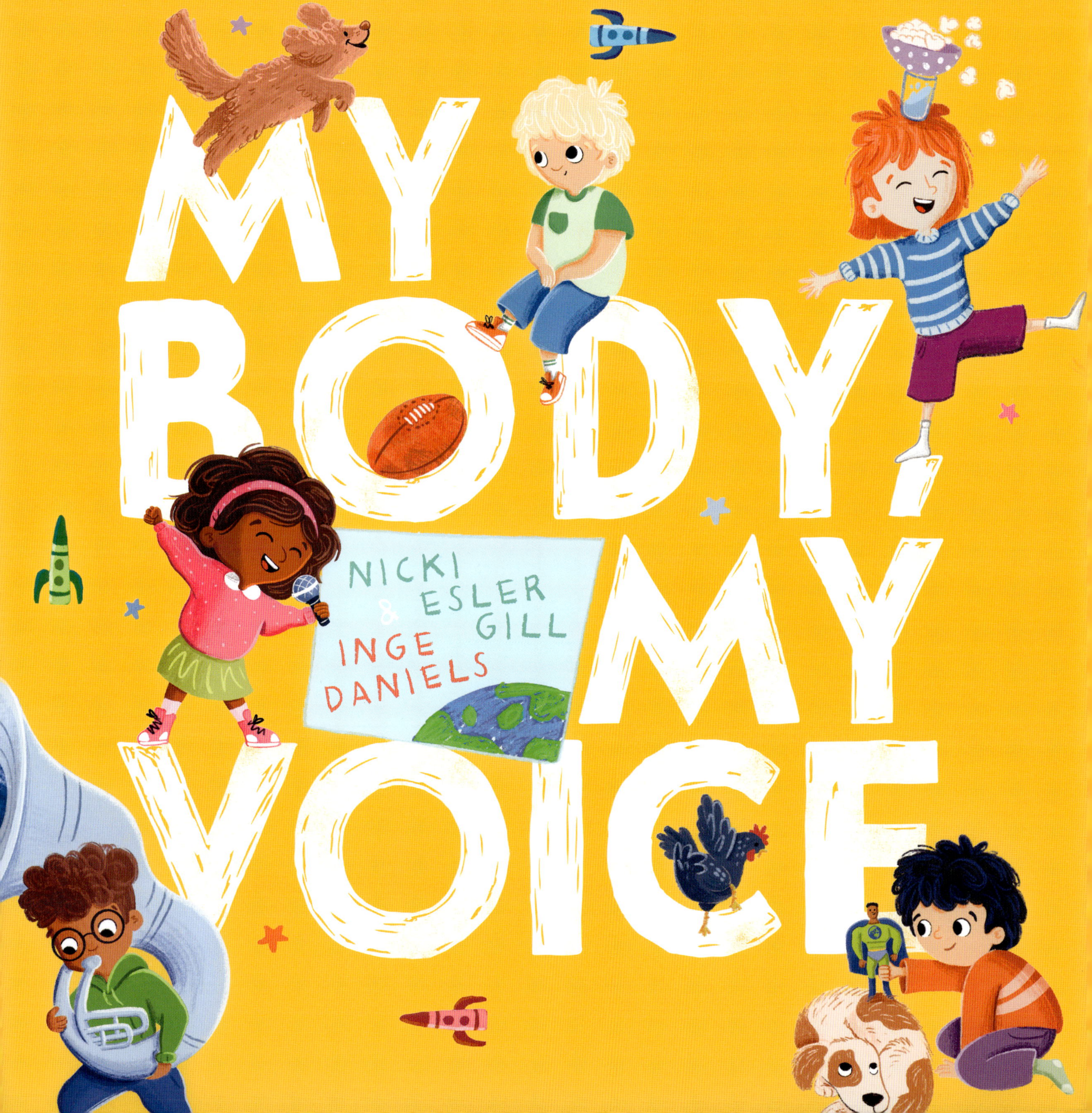

Have you ever said **'I love you'**
when your heart's all full and warm?

Have you asked to have a **cuddle**
when there's thunder in a storm?

Have you ever told your favourite joke?
Or sung a **lullaby?**

Have you poured your worries out,
and finished with a **sigh?**

Have you nattered with a cousin?
Have you hollered at the park?

Have you **whispered** at a sleepover
while lying in the dark?

Have you told yourself **'Keep trying!'**
when tying up your shoe?

Have you howled, hooted, squeaked
or crowed **'A-cock-a-doodle-doo!'**?

Have you **helped** at celebrations? Offered chips and dips and seats?

Have you bellowed, **'Mum, come look at me!'** when doing daring feats?

Have you asked
why water's wet and
dogs don't talk
and you can't fly?

Or begged for five
more minutes when it's
time to say **goodbye?**

When cheering for your teammates,
have you seen their spirits **soar**
as voices joined together
rise into a **mighty roar?**

The love that you are showing
with your voices shouting **loud**

helps their legs to whirr along,
as they run fast to make you **proud**.

Have you ever asked a **new kid**
if they want to join the game

even though you've never met before
and you don't know their **name?**

Have they said, **'Yes!'** and **'Thank you!'**?
Have they added to the fun?

And before the game is over,
they've made **friends** with everyone?

Can you see the **power** hidden
in the words you choose to say?

Your voice is **important!**
It can make somebody's day!

But think of playing all your favourite songs at the **same time**.

They'd mix to make a dreadful din. No single song could **shine**!

You wouldn't understand the words.
You wouldn't hear the **beat.**
You wouldn't feel like dancing,
even with your **dancing feet.**

So even though a noisy noise can go along with fun,
a disco party's at its best with tunes played **one by one.**

With people it's the same.
Your **voice** is like a song!

It helps to **speak and listen**
one by one, to get along.

Just like your voice matters,
others **matter** too.

So listen up and you might learn
a different **point of view**.

The voice that shouts the loudest isn't always **right.**
And brave and gentle voices have a special kind of **might.**

Like **speaking out** when something
seems important to be said.

Or talking through your worries
so they're not **stuck** in your head.

Know that you can ask for **help!** It's not all up to you!
Speak **kindly** to yourself, just like a friend would do.

It’s true you might be little.
Your muscles may be **small.**

So you might think the things you do
can’t **change** the world at all.

It's true that kids don't make the laws,
like **'toys should all be free!'**

But you can make a **difference,**
just as sure as sure can be.

For little things have power too,
and **words** you choose each day
can make the world a **better,
fairer, kinder** place to play.